AF283999

With love
Hot + Ste
Rotorua. Ur 2005

Volcanic Heartland
Rotorua · Taupo · Tongariro

CRAIG
POTTON
PUBLISHING

Bay of Plenty

Tauranga •

Hamilton •

Rotorua •
Whakarewarewa •
Lkae Okataina
Lake Tarawera
Late Rotokakahi ▲ MT TARAWERA

Te Kuiti • • Waiotapu

KAINGAROA
FOREST

Orakeikorako • TE UREWERA
NAITONAL
WHIRINAKI PARK
FOREST
PARK

PUREORA • Wairakei
FOREST • Taupo
PARK Lake
Lake Taupo Waikaremoana

Taumarunui •

▲ MT TONGARIRO

▲ MT NGAURUHOE

Whakapapa • TONGARIRO
▲ MT RUAPEHU NATIONAL
PARK

RANGIPO DESERT

Ohakune •

Hawke
Napier • Bay

INTRODUCTION

The first voyagers to the Central North Island arrived from East Polynesia aboard the Te Arawa canoe, perhaps 800-900 years ago. They made landfall at Maketu in the Bay of Plenty, after which the chief Ngatoroirangi journeyed inland. The Rotorua lakes were created in his footsteps, and he named many now familiar places - Kaimanawa, Tongariro, Ngauruhoe and Rangipo. He was the first to ascend Tongariro (now in the Tongariro National Park) which he did to claim the surrounding land on behalf of his people. But the ascent was not without suffering, and Ngatoroirangi almost froze to death. He called to his sisters in far off Hawaiiki to send heat. They responded, with the help of the fire gods Pupu and Te Hoata, who sent fire underground, creating the volcanic and thermal areas of the Central North Island in the process. On Tongariro, Ngatoroirangi cast down a sacred stone, and the land burst open as a volcano, into the crater of which he threw the body of his unfortunate slave, Ngauruhoe, as an offering of thanks to the gods who had saved him.

This myth shows a remarkable understanding of the origins of the Central North Island's volcanic and geothermal activity. In this part of the world, fire has been travelling underground and erupting in dramatic fashion over millions and millions of years. New Zealand's position on the Pacific Ring of Fire, over the boundary of two of the world's crustal plates, has generated intense heat and pressure that raised the land and began creating volcanoes 22 million years ago in northern New Zealand. Volcanic activity has slowly moved south toward what is now called the Taupo Volcanic Zone, which stretches from White Island in the east, to the most southerly expression of active volcanism in New Zealand - the volcanoes of Tongariro National Park.

This zone has been active for just two million years, and those who have unravelled its history tell of cataclysmic events that pale many better-known volcanic eruptions to insignificance. Two such eruptions occurred from the huge caldera now filled by Lake Taupo, one 30,000 years ago, the second about 2000 years ago – an event recorded in Rome and China when skies darkened and the world climate cooled. This latter eruption was 12 times bigger than Krakatoa (1883) and 30 times the size of Mt St Helens (1980). It devastated almost one-third of the North Island.

Eruptions still regularly occur on the classic andesitic volcanoes of Mts Ngauruhoe and Ruapehu, the latest being in 1995 and 1996 from Mt Ruapehu. Life threatening lahars (mudflows) have been sent down from Ruapehu's Crater Lake on many occasions in recorded memory. One tragic event killed 151 people in 1953 when a lahar destroyed a rail bridge at Tangiwai just before an express train was due. The 1886 Tarawera eruption killed a similar number of people, burying many alive in ash at the village of Te Wairoa.

Amongst its volcanoes and geothermal fields, the Central North Island bustles with economic activity. Vast areas were planted in monterey pine from the 1920s and 1930s onwards in what became the world's largest afforestation scheme – the result of a determination that native timbers would be insufficient to meet demand at some time in the ensuing 40 years. Pulp, paper and fibreboard industries flourished, and exports of these products and logs has turned Tauranga into a major port. The widespread clearance of native forests in the Central North Island was not without its flashpoints, as raised environmental consciousness in the 1970s was translated into a famous treetop protest in Pureora Forest, west of Taupo, and clashes at Whirinaki Forest, east of Taupo on the margins of Te Urewera National Park. Though the eventual preservation of these lowland conifer-broadleaf forest remnants was a far-sighted act, it was far too late for the magnificent forests that once dominated the Central North Island.

Between the 1920s and 1960s, the central North Island also experienced spectacular growth in sheep and cattle numbers, particularly when mineral deficiencies in soils derived from volcanic ash were identified and rectified. Electricity generation here has been another important aspect of the region's and the nation's development. Both the Tongariro and Waikato rivers are dammed – eight dams on the upper Waikato built between the 1920s and 1960s contribute 1045 megawatts to the national grid, while the two power stations on the Tongariro contribute 320 megawatts. Geothermal energy has been harnessed too. The 190 megawatt Wairakei station, at Wairakei, north of Taupo, was only the second geothermal station in the world when commissioned in 1963. A second 100 megawatt geothermal station, Ohaaki was opened in 1989 after extensive negotiations with the Ngati Tahu tribe to ensure protection of their marae and sacred sites.

The world famous Taupo rainbow trout fishery attracts thousands to the region's lakes and rivers each year. Similarly, Rotorua's numerous accessible geothermal attractions and Maori cultural activities have made this city one of the country's most important tourist destinations. Winter skiers and summer walkers go to Tongariro

National Park to enjoy its recreational offerings. The day-long Tongariro Crossing of Mt Tongariro is one of New Zealand's most popular walking excursions through a variety of volcanic features, from hot springs to steaming craters, and emerald-coloured lakes. Walks among the ancient trees of Pureora and Whirinaki forest parks are further off the tourist trails, but no less rewarding.

Maori reverence for the volatile Central North Island landscape remains undiminished. The volcanoes, lakes, and rivers are powerful sources of tribal mana, and conflict between Maori and Pakeha when sacred sites have been at risk of desecration has been a common feature of the last 150 years. But one of the most remarkable acts in the history of Maori-Pakeha relations occurred in 1887 when the paramount chief of Ngati Tuwharetoa gifted the sacred Tongariro volcanoes to the Government. 'The Gift' led to the creation of the New Zealand's first national park – Tongariro – which was then only the fourth national park in the world. Just over 100 years later the park was granted World Heritage status, not just for its outstanding natural landscape values, but also for its outstanding cultural values – the first area in the world to be given this dual recognition.

(Previous page) Rotorua's Pohutu Geyser, the largest in New Zealand which reaches heights of 31 m.
(Right) Mt Ruapehu, photographed near Ohakune.

Sun rises on the sacred peaks of Tongariro National Park
(left): Tongariro (obscured by cloud in the foreground), the
classic andesitic cone Ngauruhoe, and the Mt Ruapehu massif
in the distance. In the dead of winter snow falls to low levels
on Mt Ruapehu, coating the beech forest near Whakapapa
(top). In spring and early summer alpine flowers emerge,
including the sun orchid *Thelymitra decora* (above). Mt
Ruapehu erupts (overleaf) in June 1996.

Forests on sheltered western and southern slopes of Ruapehu (opposite page) were the only ones to survive the Taupo eruption almost 2000 years ago. Podocarp species such as the kahikatea pictured survive in small pockets, but the predominant tree in Tongariro National Park is beech. The mountain cabbage tree *Cordyline indivisa* (top) in beech forest on Mt Ruapehu. Water falls over a lava flow at Soda Springs (left) flanked by yellow-flowering buttercups, mountain foxgloves and tussock grasses.

Sunrise over a shattered volcanic landscape (overleaf): Tongariro's Blue Lake in the foreground, and Mts Ngauruhoe and Ruapehu.

The walk across Mt Tongariro is one of the world's finest day treks. Much of the higher part of the route is seen in the photo opposite – a landscape of lava flows, active craters, steaming vents, hot springs and emerald-coloured lakes. Tongariro's Red Crater (foreground, opposite page) is still considered active. It last erupted in 1925. Among the highlights of the walk are the mineral-rich 'Emerald' Lakes (top) that fill small pit craters. The buttercup *Ranunculus insignis* (above) grows in alpine areas throughout the park.

is surprisingly diverse. Near the summit of Ruapehu, the Crater Lake (far left) simmers in the aftermath of a powerful series of eruptions which in 1996 emptied the lake for the second time in a century. The lake is one of just three such crater lakes in the world. Mangahuehu Hut on the southwestern side of Ruapehu (left), on the popular round-the-mountain track, a 5–6 day tramp.

Mt Ruapehu and the Rangipo Desert (top) in eastern Tongariro National Park. The desert is layered metres deep with ash, volcanic mudflows (lahars) lava and 'bombs' – rocks ejected from the volcanoes. Despite poor soils and a severe climate, the desert ecology

Two views from the trail across Mt Tongariro: The Emerald Lakes (top), and the vista north from near Ketetahi Springs toward Lake Rotaira, and Lake Taupo in the far distance (above). Between the lakes is the dome formed by Mt Pihanga, in Maori folklore the maiden over whom the central North Island volcanoes fought before Taranaki was driven off to the West Coast. Stunning tracts of native tussock grasslands lie between Ngauruhoe and Mt Ruapehu (left). Forests have struggled to colonise the area, stymied by eruptions and fires, allowing tussock grasses to become established.

Lake Taupo, the scene about 2000 years ago of one of the world's most devastating volcanic eruptions, pictured here in quiescent mood. Most evenings and early mornings draw fly fishermen to the mouths of rivers feeding the lake (above). Since first stocked with introduced rainbow trout last century, the lake has become a renowned fishery. Set against the backdrop of the Tongariro volcanoes, both lake and district (opposite page) are important tourist and holiday destinations.

The 425 km long Waikato River begins indistinctly on eastern Ruapehu and flows into Lake Taupo as the Tongariro River, re-emerging as the lake's major outlet at Taupo. Just north of Taupo the full flow of the river is channelled into the 15 m chasm at the top of Huka Falls (opposite page), an 11 m drop run by the occasional brave kayaker. Aratiatia Rapids (above), 10 km downstream of Huka Falls offers challenging whitewater, and was recently the venue for a world kayaking championship. There are eight hydro dams on the river between Taupo and Karapiro.

Kayaking on Lake Taupo (previous page), with the western shores and cliffs of Whanganui Bay in the distance.

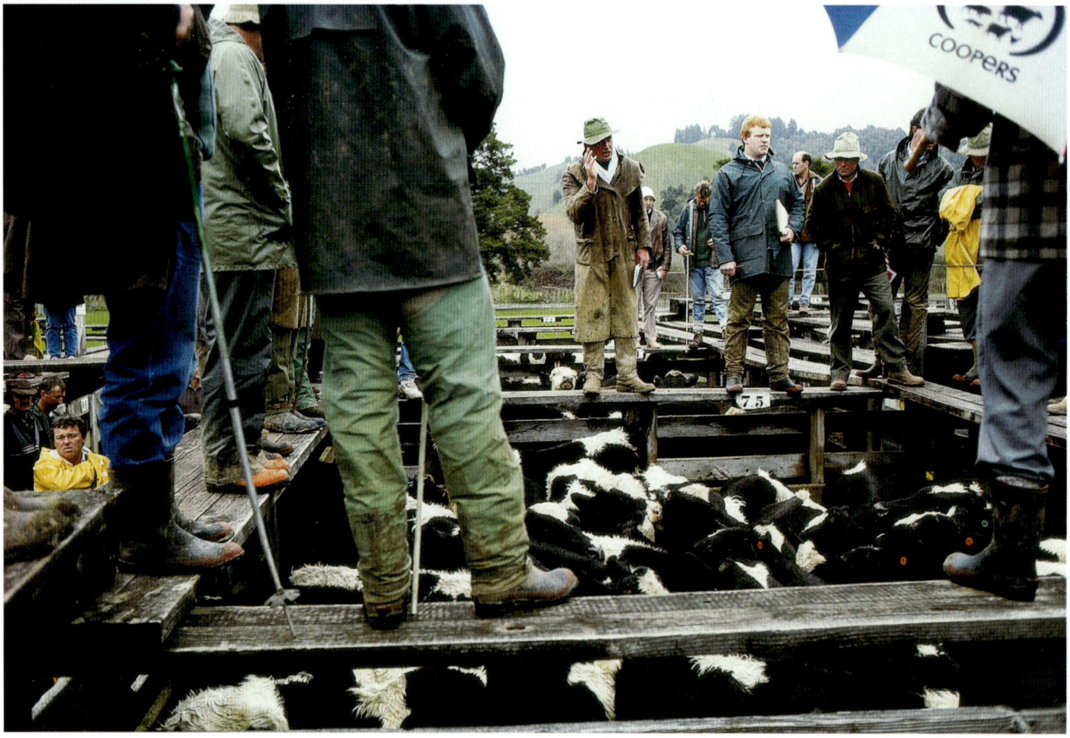
COOPERS
7.5

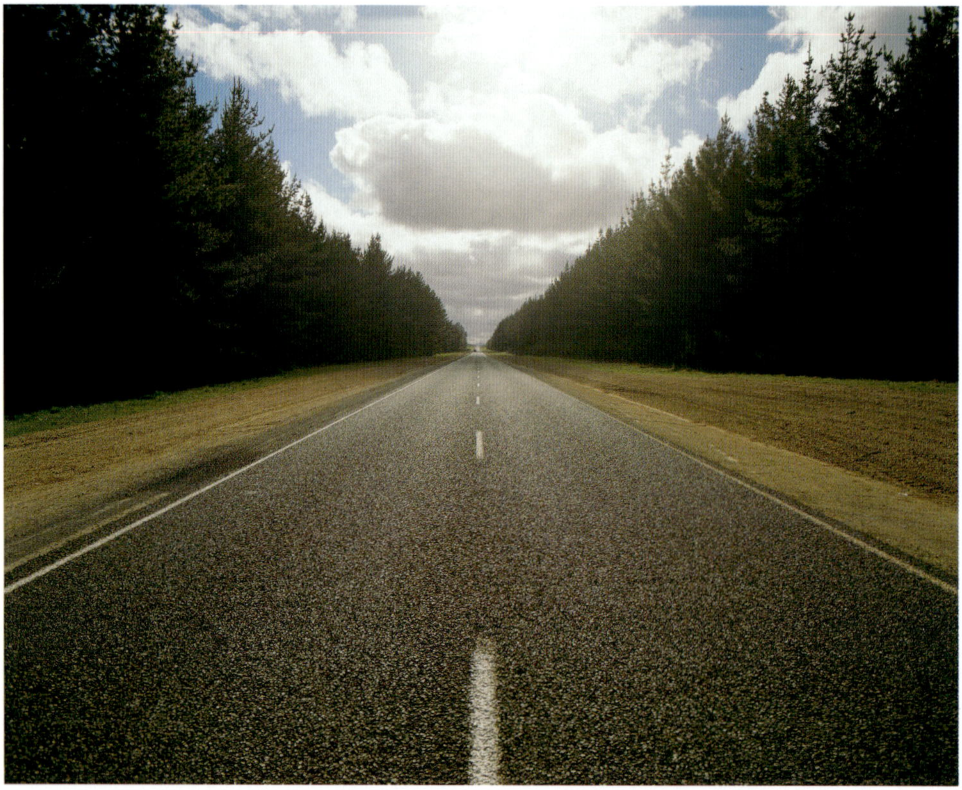

Four Central North Island industries (clockwise from left): the Craters of the Moon geothermal area, one of the Taupo district's important tourist attractions; Kaingaroa Forest, part of the world's largest afforestation scheme, pictured on the Taupo-Rotorua highway; A stock sale at Taumarunui, still an important aspect of Waikato's traditional rural economy; The Wairakei geothermal power station was just the second in the world when it was commissioned.

Rotorua's treasure chest of geothermal attractions offers treats for visitor and scientist alike. The main feature of the Waiotapu thermal reserve, 34 km southeast of Rotorua is the Champagne Pool (above and opposite page). Thought to be about 900 years old, the 2000 sq m pool was formed by hydrothermal explosions that allowed chloride water to flood the pool. Mineral deposits have since provided the pool's spectacular colouring. The Lady Knox Geyser (left) is set off everyday at 10.30 am with soap! Waiotapu means 'sacred waters'.

Three images from the Waimangu thermal area, 26 km southeast of Rotorua: Warbrick Terrace (above), a gaudily coloured geothermal formation; steam emerges from fissures in the Cathedral Rocks (left); the Waimangu Cauldron (far left) formed during an eruption in 1917, is one of the world's largest boiling lakes. Several features at Waimangu were formed by the Tarawera eruption in 1886, including Raumoko's Throat and a number of craters.

Clockwise from left: Fumaroles on a silica terrace at Orakeikorako thermal area; the 7 km rent in Mt Tarawera formed by the 1886 eruption that killed 153 people, most of them buried, at nearby Te Wairoa; Sinter terraces at Waimangu thermal area.

Saved from the chainsaw after a bitter conservation confrontation in the 1970s, Whirinaki Forest Park (above and opposite page), like Pureora Forest, west of Lake Taupo, is a small remnant of the vast conifer-broadleaf forest that once covered the Central North Island. Located south-east of Rotorua off SH 38 to Lake Waikaremoana, Whirinaki forest contains startlingly beautiful tall trees. The spectacular Tree Trunk Gorge (left) in the Kaimanawa Range was formed as the Tongariro River cut through volcanic ignimbrite.

Whakarewarewa is Rotorua's best known thermal area and has been a significant tourist attraction for more than a century. The Whakarewarewa valley was formed about 42,000 years ago, and today features mudpools, boiling water, geysers (such as the Prince of Wales Feathers, left), steam vents (above), and places to bathe (opposite page). When rainwater percolates through the surface it is super-heated by magma and forced back to the surface, emerging in often spectacular forms. The Pohutu Geyser (see page 5) is the area's largest geyser, reaching heights of more than 30 m.

As well as its thermal attractions, Whakarewarewa is an important cultural centre. The Whakarewarewa Valley has long been home to the Ngatiwhakaue tribe, and today the pallisaded model village with buildings and structures typical of pre-European pa (above) is part of an important tourism venture run by the tribe. For many tourists, Whakarewarewa offers a first glimpse of Maori culture. Haka are performed for visitors (right), who can also watch carvers at work at the village's arts and crafts institute (far right).

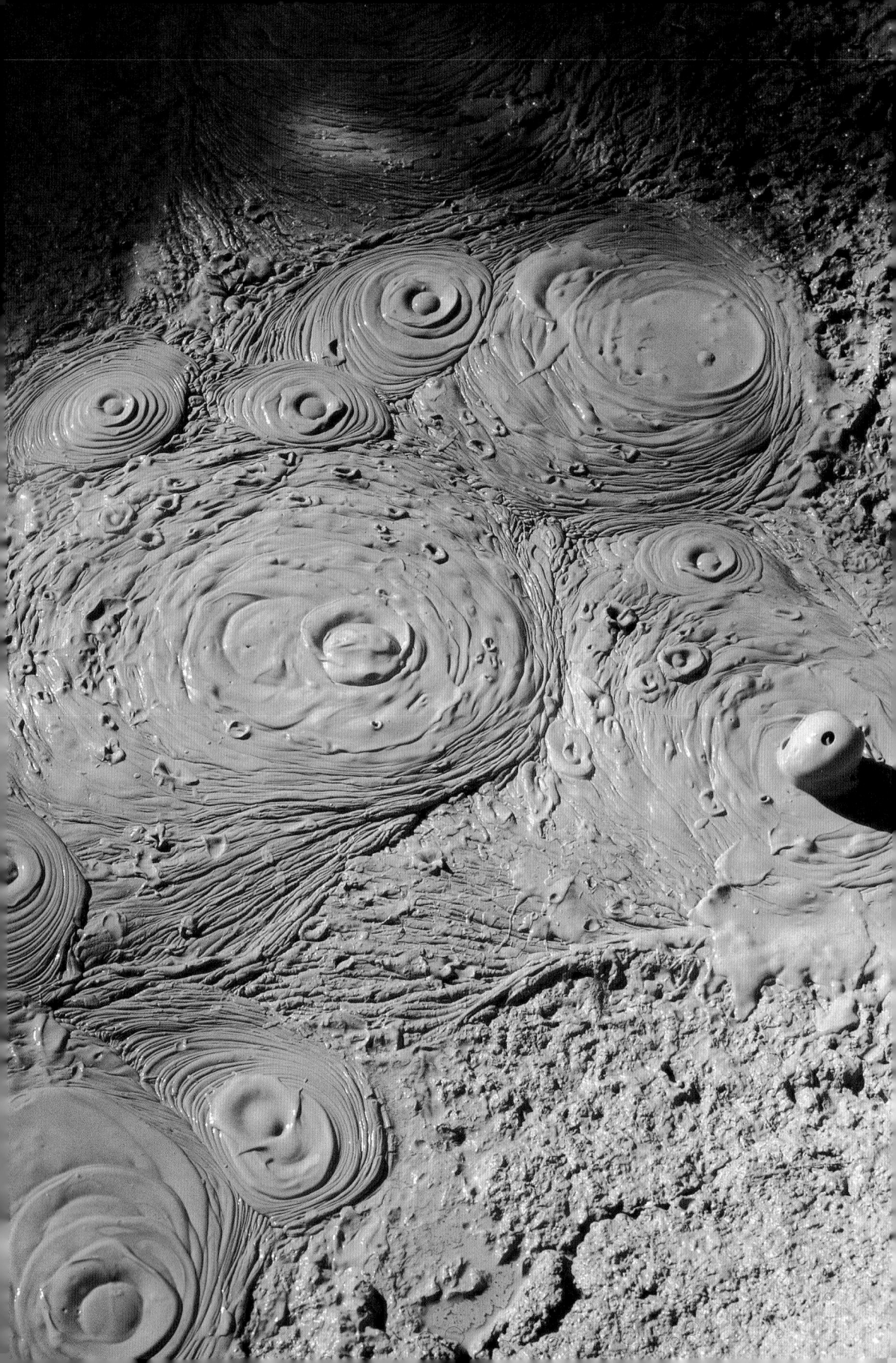

The exterior of Whakarewarewa's wharenui (meeting house) is adorned with carvings (above), while inside intricate kowhaiwhai patterns decorate roof beams (left). The wharenui is the central focus of any Maori marae (meeting place), and carvings and paintings often depict tribal lineage and history. Some mudpool trivia: mudpools (opposite page) change in consistency according to the season. In summer, as in this photo, the mud is thicker because there is less rainwater.

Tranquil Lake Okareka (left) is one of a string of beautiful lakes with high natural and cultural values east of Rotorua. The waters of Okareka, Okataina, Tikitapu, Rotokakahi and Tarawera all fill ancient caldera active tens of thousands of years ago. They are especially revered by the Te Arawa tribe who are likely to be offered the lakes in a settlement with the Government in the near future. Te Wairoa Falls (above) cascades down a fissure near Te Wairoa, the location of a village that was buried by the 1886 eruption of Mt Tarawera.

Rotorua's museum and art gallery in Government Gardens (above) was formerly an upscale bathhouse which, like many buildings and homes, was plumbed into the natural water heater bubbling away just under the city's surface. The gallery's ostentatious Elizabethan Tudor architecture was supposed to mimic nineteenth century European spas (a dip in a natural hot water pool is still possible at a number of places in the city). Drawing on its Maori heritage, Rotorua is also a place to indulge in indigenous arts and crafts – the making of a flax kete (basket) is an art still practised according to traditional standards (left). Rainbow Springs (far left) trout hatchery is the place to see rainbow trout close up.

All photography by Craig Potton except:
David Wall pgs 20/21, 22
Shaun Barnett/Black Robin Photography pgs 14/15, 24/25
Brian Moorhead/Focus New Zealand Photo Library p. 44/45
Grant Burns/Photosource p. 42
Bruce Foster/Photosource pgs 40/41
Cliff Threadgold/Photosource p. 23 bottom

Text: Dave Chowdhury
Printing: Printlink, Wellington, New Zealand

First published in 2001 by Craig Potton Publishing
© 2001 Craig Potton Publishing
© Individual photographers

ISBN 0 908802 82 X

All rights reserved. No part of this publication may be reproduced, stored
in a retrieval system, or transmitted in any form, or by any means,
electronic, mechanical, photocopying, recording, or otherwise, without
prior written permission from the publisher.